INSIDE THE NFL

SEATTLE SEAHAWKS

BY TODD RYAN

SportsZone
An Imprint of Abdo Publishing
abdobooks.com

abdobooks.com

Published by Abdo Publishing, a division of ABDO, PO Box 398166, Minneapolis, Minnesota 55439.

Printed in the United States of America, North Mankato, Minnesota
022019
092019

THIS BOOK CONTAINS
RECYCLED MATERIALS

Cover Photo: Elaine Thompson/AP Images
Interior Photos: Kevin Terrell/AP Images, 4–5; Paul Kitagaki Jr./The Sacramento Bee/AP Images, 6; Matt Slocum/AP Images, 9; NFL Photos/AP Images, 11, 12, 15, 21; Peter Read Miller/AP Images, 16; Al Messerschmidt/AP Images, 19, 22; Barry Sweet/AP Images, 24, 43; Bill Haber/AP Images, 27; Cheryl Hatch/AP Images, 29; Ben Margot/AP Images, 31; John Froschauer/AP Images, 32; John Medina/Getty Images Sport/Getty Images, 35; Ted S. Warren/AP Images, 36; David J Phillip/AP Images, 40

Editor: Patrick Donnelly
Series Designer: Craig Hinton

Library of Congress Control Number: 2018966005

Publisher's Cataloging-in-Publication Data

Names: Ryan, Todd, author.
Title: Seattle Seahawks / by Todd Ryan
Description: Minneapolis, Minnesota: Abdo Publishing, 2020 | Series: Inside the NFL | Includes online resources and index.
Identifiers: ISBN 9781532118647 (lib. bdg.) | ISBN 9781532172823 (ebook) | ISBN 9781644941164 (pbk.)
Subjects: LCSH: Seattle Seahawks (Football team)--Juvenile literature. | National Football League--Juvenile literature. | Football teams--Juvenile literature. | American football--Juvenile literature.
Classification: DDC 796.33264--dc23

TABLE OF CONTENTS

CHAPTER 1

SUPER SEAHAWKS

Seattle Seahawks fans were hungry for a Super Bowl title heading into the 2013 season. The team had been members of the National Football League (NFL) for nearly 40 years and had never won the league title. But the pieces were in place to win it all in 2013.

The Seahawks put together a 13–3 regular season, a record good enough to earn home-field advantage throughout the National Football Conference (NFC) playoffs. This was big for the Seahawks, whose home stadium is one of the loudest in the league. The fans make so much noise that small earthquakes have been detected after particularly loud outbursts.

Seattle's raucous fans give the Seahawks an incredible home-field advantage.

LOUDER!

Richard Sherman, *right*, keeps Michael Crabtree from catching a potential game-winning touchdown pass in the NFC Championship Game.

The Seahawks gave their fans plenty to cheer about in January 2014. They opened the playoffs with a 23–15 win over the New Orleans Saints. That meant they would host the NFC Championship Game. Their opponent was their biggest rival—the San Francisco 49ers. Both teams came in with strong defenses and quarterbacks who were dangerous throwing or running with the ball.

The game was a tough, physical battle typical of the growing rivalry. The Niners took leads of 10–0 and 17–10, but the Seahawks pulled ahead 20–17 in the fourth quarter when quarterback Russell Wilson connected with wide receiver Jermaine Kearse on a 35-yard touchdown pass.

Seattle added another field goal, leaving San Francisco one last chance. Trailing 23–17 with 3:32 to play, the Niners took over on their own 22-yard line. Quarterback Colin Kaepernick led them down the field quickly. The 49ers reached the Seattle 18-yard line with 30 seconds to play. A touchdown would give them a chance to kick a game-winning extra point.

That's when Seahawks cornerback Richard Sherman made the play of the game. Kaepernick tried to find receiver Michael Crabtree in the corner of the end zone. Sherman jumped high, reached back with his left hand, and tipped the ball away from Crabtree and directly to linebacker Malcolm Smith, who made the interception to save the game.

In the Super Bowl, Seattle would face the Denver Broncos and legendary quarterback Peyton Manning. The Broncos had just set an NFL record for most points scored in a season. But Seattle's defense was up to the challenge.

In fact, the Seahawks took a 2–0 lead just 12 seconds into the game. The Broncos' first snap to Manning went over the quarterback's head. Denver scrambled to get the ball back and make sure Seattle didn't recover it for a touchdown. The Broncos fell on the ball in the end zone, but the safety gave the Seahawks the lead for good.

The Seattle defense made life miserable for Manning all game. After the Seahawks' offense managed field goals on its first two possessions, safety Kam Chancellor intercepted Manning in Denver territory. Four minutes later, running back Marshawn Lynch scored from the 1-yard line and Seattle led 15–0.

RUSSELL WILSON

The Seahawks selected Russell Wilson in the third round of the 2012 NFL Draft. He was slated to back up starter Matt Flynn. But head coach Pete Carroll saw something in Wilson. The rookie beat out Flynn, who had signed a huge free-agent contract in the offseason to become the Seahawks starting quarterback. NFL fans voted Wilson the 2012 NFL Rookie of the Year, and in his second season, he led Seattle to its first Super Bowl title.

Even when things went right for Denver, it didn't last. The Broncos drove methodically across the 50-yard line and into Seattle territory. Then Manning's arm was hit as he tried to pass. The ball fluttered in the air and Smith stepped in front of the Denver receiver for another big interception. Smith raced 69 yards untouched for a Seahawks touchdown and a 22–0 lead. When Seattle's Percy Harvin returned the

Super Bowl MVP Malcolm Smith celebrates with the Lombardi Trophy.

opening kickoff of the second half for a touchdown, the game was as good as over.

In the end, the game was one of the biggest blowouts in Super Bowl history. The Seahawks ended up winning 43–8. As the seconds ticked down, the players dumped Gatorade on head coach Pete Carroll and the celebration was on. Smith ended up being named the game's Most Valuable Player (MVP), and for the first time ever, the Seattle Seahawks were Super Bowl champions.

CHAPTER 2

REACHING THE "BIG TIME"

Seattle was hungry for a professional football team. On December 5, 1974, the wish of the city's residents came true. At a news conference in New York, NFL commissioner Pete Rozelle announced that Seattle had been awarded a franchise. The efforts of Lloyd W. Nordstrom and the Seattle Professional Football ownership group had paid off.

The city had hoped to land a pro football team. So construction had started on the Kingdome in 1972, before Seattle even had a team. The Seahawks began play in the dome in 1976, their first NFL season.

John Thompson was hired as the Seahawks' general manager. He hired the team's first head coach, Jack Patera. Patera had played in the NFL as a linebacker for three teams.

Seattle quarterback Jim Zorn scrambles for extra yardage during the Seahawks' first NFL victory in October 1976.

The Seahawks' first head coach, Jack Patera, watches from the sideline during a game in 1976.

He also had served as an assistant coach with the Los Angeles Rams, the New York Giants, and the Minnesota Vikings.

However, the Seahawks' original owner would never even see the team play a game. Nordstrom died suddenly of a heart attack on January 20, 1976, while vacationing in Mexico. His brother Elmer took over as the Seahawks' owner.

The Seahawks joined the league with the Tampa Bay Buccaneers. In March 1976 the two new teams took turns making picks from lists of players made available by the existing NFL teams. The Seahawks wound up selecting 39 players in the expansion draft. The regular NFL Draft, involving standout college players, was later that spring. The Seahawks chose defensive lineman Steve Niehaus from the University of Notre Dame as their first draft pick. He was taken second overall and became the 1976 NFC Defensive Rookie of the Year.

THE FIRST COACH

Jack Patera was chosen as the Seahawks' first head coach after the team considered more than a dozen other candidates. He was not very well known before his arrival in Seattle, as he had spent his career as an assistant coach in the NFL. In his six full seasons with the Seahawks, Patera never led them to the playoffs. He finished his career with a 35–59 record.

Seattle discovered two of its greatest players in unconventional ways in 1976. Quarterback Jim Zorn was an undrafted free agent. He made such an impact in his first season that he was named the NFC Offensive Rookie of the Year. The Houston Oilers drafted wide receiver Steve Largent in 1976. But he was traded to the Seahawks for an eighth-round draft pick before the season began. He soon became Zorn's favorite target.

As the first season approached, the city was buzzing with excitement. However, the Seahawks roster was mostly made up of rookies or veteran players whom other teams did not want. The Seahawks went 1–5 in exhibition play in 1976. But the fans did not seem to mind. They could not wait for the regular season to start. A crowd of 58,441 packed into the Kingdome for the opener against the St. Louis Cardinals on September 12, 1976.

The Seahawks trailed 13–3 at halftime, and the Cardinals stretched their lead to 30–10 early in the fourth quarter. Then Zorn hooked up with wide receiver Sam McCullum on a 72-yard scoring strike. Zorn rushed 8 yards for another touchdown. The late scores pumped new life into the crowd. Although Seattle ended up losing 30–24, the fans did not go home disappointed.

It took six weeks for the Seahawks to earn their first NFL win. They traveled to Florida and beat their expansion mates in Tampa Bay 13–10 on October 17. The Seahawks won only one other game that season, defeating the Atlanta Falcons 30–13 at the Kingdome on November 7. Seattle finished its first season with a 2–12 record.

With the second overall pick in the 1977 NFL Draft, the Seahawks had a chance to acquire an impact player. But they decided that their roster needed more help than one great player could provide, so they traded their first-round pick to

Zorn and wide receiver Steve Largent talk during Seattle's 13–10 win over Tampa Bay on October 17, 1976.

Dallas for the Cowboys' first-round selection (No. 14 overall) and three second-round choices. Seattle used those picks on players who helped provide depth, while Dallas used the second overall pick to draft Tony Dorsett. The Heisman Trophy–winning running back out of the University of Pittsburgh went on to become a Hall of Famer and helped the Cowboys win the Super Bowl his rookie season.

Largent makes a catch against the Raiders in Seattle's 17–16 upset on November 26, 1978.

The Seahawks moved from the NFC West to the American Football Conference (AFC) West before the start of the 1977 season. Seattle lost its first four games before beating Tampa Bay 30–23. Two weeks later, Zorn returned from an injury and threw four touchdown passes in a 56–17 rout of the Buffalo Bills at the Kingdome. The Seahawks finished the season 5–9.

In 1978, the Seahawks started 6–6 before stunning the Raiders 17–16 in Oakland. The Seahawks' Efren Herrera made

MAKING A NAME FOR HIMSELF

Steve Largent was an All-American at the University of Tulsa but was hardly a top NFL prospect. The Houston Oilers selected him in the fourth round of the 1976 NFL Draft. After four preseason games, Houston traded him to Seattle.

Largent made the most of the opportunity with the Seahawks. He had 54 catches as a rookie. By his third season, he caught 71 passes and reached 1,000 receiving yards for the first time. He hit the 1,000-yard mark in seven more seasons during his career.

Largent was not terribly fast, but he had great hands. He spent 14 seasons with the Seahawks and racked up more than 13,000 receiving yards. Largent was selected to seven Pro Bowls and was inducted into the Pro Football Hall of Fame in 1995.

a 46-yard field goal with three seconds left. It marked the first time in 13 years that any team had defeated Oakland twice in one season. Largent had 1,168 receiving yards that season and helped Seattle finish with its first winning record, 9–7. Largent earned a spot in the Pro Bowl, and Patera was named the NFL Coach of the Year.

In 1979 the Seahawks lost four of their first five games but recovered nicely for their first *Monday Night Football* contest. Seattle edged host Atlanta 31–28. That victory provided a shot of momentum for the Seahawks. They won five of their final seven games to finish 9–7 again. Hope for the future was bright.

CHAPTER 3

BECOMING A CONTENDER

The Seahawks were coming off back-to-back winning seasons going into 1980. However, they failed to build on the momentum. Seattle lost its final eight games of the year to finish 4–12. The next year, Steve Largent racked up 1,224 receiving yards, but he could not save the Seahawks from losing six of their first seven games and finishing 6–10.

Jack Patera was fired after the Seahawks lost their first two games of the 1982 season. A players' strike wiped out seven games over the next two months. When the NFL returned to action, Seattle had a new coach. Director of football operations Mike McCormack filled in on a temporary basis. The Seahawks finished with a 4–5 record, and

Quarterback Dave Krieg helped the Seahawks make the playoffs four times in the 1980s.

SEIZING AN OPPORTUNITY

Dave Krieg did not enter the NFL with much hype. He had been the seventh-string quarterback at one point at tiny Milton College in Wisconsin. He was given a chance to play in the fourth game of his freshman season. Three of his four completions went for touchdowns. He was named the starter for the rest of the season. Krieg's head coach was so impressed as Krieg's career went on that he wrote a letter to the Seahawks and sent game film to the team.

Krieg earned a tryout with the Seahawks after college and made the team in 1980. He spent 12 seasons in Seattle, throwing for 195 touchdowns with just 148 interceptions. Krieg was selected to three Pro Bowls, all while he was a Seahawk. He played 19 seasons overall in the NFL with six teams.

McCormack returned to the front office after the season as president and general manager.

The team welcomed new coach Chuck Knox in 1983. Knox had coached the Los Angeles Rams and the Buffalo Bills. He turned Seattle into a contender.

A change took place at quarterback as well, with Dave Krieg replacing Jim Zorn after eight games. A thrilling 51–48 overtime win over the Kansas City Chiefs in the Kingdome improved the Seahawks' record to 7–6. Seattle finished 9–7, clinching its first playoff berth in team history with a 24–6 win over the New England Patriots in the last game of the season.

Chuck Knox led the Seahawks to four playoff appearances between 1983 and 1991.

Krieg proved himself in his postseason debut, a wild-card game against the Denver Broncos. In a Christmas Eve showdown with quarterback John Elway at the Kingdome, Krieg threw three touchdown passes as the Seahawks smashed the Broncos 31–7.

A trip to the Orange Bowl for a divisional-round game against quarterback Dan Marino and the Miami Dolphins was next for the Seahawks. The Dolphins went 12–4 in the regular season and were the defending AFC champions.

Curt Warner carries the ball in Seattle's AFC playoff game at Miami on December 31, 1983.

With 3:43 remaining in the game, it seemed as if Miami was in control. Seattle trailed 20–17 but refused to give up. Krieg ignited a rally with passes of 16 and 40 yards to Largent.

Then rookie running back Curt Warner plunged 2 yards for a touchdown and a 24–20 Seahawks advantage.

Seattle forced a fumble on the ensuing kickoff and recovered the ball. A field goal capped the 27–20 victory and lifted the Seahawks into the AFC Championship Game against the Los Angeles Raiders. That's where their first playoff trip ended. The Raiders blasted the Seahawks 30–14 in Los Angeles on the way to winning the Super Bowl.

REMARKABLE ROOKIE SEASON

Curt Warner did not need much time to excel with the Seahawks. Fresh off a senior season at Penn State University in which he led the Nittany Lions to a national title, Warner continued his strong play as a rookie in the NFL. He was the No. 3 overall pick in the 1983 NFL Draft. As a rookie, he ran for 1,449 yards and scored 14 touchdowns (13 rushing, one receiving). His stellar season helped the Seahawks march into the playoffs for the first time in team history.

The Seahawks rode their momentum to 12 wins in their first 14 games in the 1984 season. Seattle was successful despite losing Warner to a season-ending knee injury in Week 1. Krieg made up the difference. He threw for 3,671 yards and a career high 32 touchdowns.

Seattle lost to visiting Denver 31–14 in the regular-season finale and finished with a 12–4 record. The Broncos won the

Seattle's Jacob Green, *right*, sacks Raiders quarterback Jim Plunkett in the Seahawks' 1984 playoff victory at the Kingdome.

AFC West. The Seahawks had to settle for a wild-card berth in the postseason.

In their playoff opener, the Seahawks faced the Raiders in a rematch, this time in the Kingdome. Seattle forced three turnovers and beat Los Angeles 13–7. A week later, the season ended in another playoff rematch, with Miami getting revenge in a 31–10 blowout.

Seattle missed the playoffs at 8–8 in 1985 and again in 1986 despite a 10–6 finish. The Seahawks returned to the postseason by going 9–6 in a strike-shortened 1987 season. The trip did not last long, though. The Seahawks lost 23–20 in overtime at Houston.

Krieg separated his shoulder early in the 1988 season. The team struggled while Krieg was out. When he returned, Seattle finished strong and captured its first AFC West title.

A playoff run was not in the cards, however. The host Cincinnati Bengals beat the Seahawks 21–13 in the divisional round. It would be the last postseason appearance for Seattle for a decade. The Seahawks went 7–9 in 1989 to close out the 1980s.

A SAVIOR IN SEATTLE

Chuck Knox took over as coach in Seattle at a time when the city's excitement for the team was dying down. The fans were tired of the team being average and wanted to see a winner on the field. Knox delivered. He led the Seahawks into the playoffs during his first season and almost guided them to the Super Bowl. Knox won 83 games, including three in the playoffs, in his time as Seahawks coach, from 1983 to 1991.

CHAPTER 4

SAD TIMES IN SEATTLE

Seattle finished a respectable 9–7 in 1990. But it missed out on a trip to the playoffs. There seemed to be hope in 1991 when the team chose quarterback Dan McGwire with the sixteenth pick in the NFL Draft.

McGwire, younger brother of pro baseball slugger Mark McGwire, was supposed to be the team's quarterback of the future. However, the ex-San Diego State University star spent most of his rookie season on the sideline. The Seahawks went 7–9, and Chuck Knox resigned as coach after the season. Tom Flores, who led the Raiders to a pair of Super Bowl championships, was named the new head coach.

McGwire only played in two games the next year and threw three interceptions. He failed to throw a touchdown

Quarterback Rick Mirer could not lead the Seahawks to a winning record in his time with them, from 1993 to 1996.

pass, and the entire team scored only 140 points during a miserable 2–14 season.

One bright spot was defensive tackle Cortez Kennedy, a rising star. He was in his third season in 1992 and had 14 sacks. He was named the league's Defensive Player of the Year.

Hope returned in 1993 as Seattle drafted Notre Dame quarterback Rick Mirer with the second pick overall. Seattle went 6–10, but Mirer was named the AFC Rookie of the Year after throwing for more than 2,800 yards and 12 touchdowns.

NOT THE NEXT MONTANA

Rick Mirer was a standout quarterback at the University of Notre Dame, just like San Francisco 49ers star Joe Montana. But the similarities ended there. Mirer played eight seasons in the NFL. Four of those years were spent in Seattle. His most successful season with the Seahawks was in 1993, when he was named the AFC Rookie of the Year. Mirer threw for 2,833 yards and 12 touchdowns with 17 interceptions that season.

It was downhill from there. Seattle never won more than eight games in a season between 1994 and 1996. After a 7–9 season in 1996, the Seahawks released Mirer.

Veteran NFL quarterback Warren Moon was a former standout at the University of Washington in Seattle. Moon was called upon to revive the Seahawks in 1997. He passed

Defensive tackle Cortez Kennedy was a standout for the Seahawks in the 1990s. He made the Pro Bowl eight times during that decade.

for 3,678 yards and 25 touchdowns, earning a Pro Bowl berth at age 41. But a four-game losing streak near the end of the season left the team at 8–8 and out of the playoffs.

Paul Allen, cofounder of the Microsoft computer corporation, bought the team before the 1997 season. He was eager to make changes. Before the start of the 1998 season, he gave head coach Dennis Erickson an ultimatum to either make the playoffs or lose his job.

The Seahawks seemed to be on the right track when they won their first three games. Moon was injured, though, and Seattle turned to backup quarterback Jon Kitna. Seattle ended up 8–8 again. Erickson was fired. Mike Holmgren, who had coached the 1996 Green Bay Packers to a Super Bowl title, was brought in to handle the general manager and head coaching duties for the Seahawks in 1999.

Seattle fed off Holmgren's enthusiasm. Kitna had a breakout season. He threw for more than 3,000 yards. He helped the Seahawks win eight of their first 10 games. He also won the respect of his teammates.

The Seahawks struggled near the end of the season and lost five of their final six games. They still managed to win the AFC West and make their first trip to the playoffs in 11 years. The Seahawks played host to Miami in the first round of the playoffs, where quarterback Dan Marino haunted them one last time. He led the Dolphins on a game-winning touchdown drive in the fourth quarter to give Miami a 20–17 win in his last playoff victory and the final game ever in the Kingdome.

With the Seahawks' new stadium still being built, the team spent the 2000 and 2001 seasons playing at the University of Washington's Husky Stadium. Seattle traded for quarterback

Quarterback Jon Kitna signed with Seattle in 1997 as an undrafted free agent. Two years later, he led the Seahawks to the playoffs.

Matt Hasselbeck before the 2001 season. Hasselbeck had been drafted by Green Bay in 1998, when Holmgren was the Packers' coach.

The Seahawks also signed veteran Trent Dilfer, the starting quarterback on the Baltimore Ravens' Super Bowl–winning team the previous season. He was expected to provide depth in case Hasselbeck struggled. Dilfer won in all four of his starts in 2001 with the Seahawks. Second-year running back Shaun Alexander also began to emerge. In a Sunday night game in November against the Oakland Raiders, Alexander rushed for

Mike Holmgren brought Seattle hope when he was hired as coach and general manager in 1999.

266 yards in a 34–27 win. Seattle finished 9–7 but again missed the playoffs.

The 2001 season was the last time Seattle played in the AFC. The NFL made divisional changes before the start of the 2002 season with the addition of a thirty-second team, the expansion Houston Texans. The Seahawks ended up in the NFC West Division.

There was excitement in the air as the Seahawks prepared to play their first season at their new home field. But Seattle lost its first regular-season game at home in 2002, falling to the Arizona Cardinals 24–13. The Seahawks lost five of their first six games. Hasselbeck did his best to revive their playoff hopes, throwing for more than 3,000 yards in 10 starts. But their slow start doomed the Seahawks to a 7–9 finish.

The tide began to turn in 2003, when Seattle went unbeaten at home, finished 10–6, and earned a wild-card playoff berth. The Seahawks traveled to Wisconsin to face Green Bay in a playoff opener at chilly Lambeau Field. Seattle rallied late and sent the game to overtime tied 27–27. But Hasselbeck threw an interception that was returned for a touchdown, ending Seattle's season.

In 2004, the Seahawks won the NFC West title. In the opening round of the playoffs, the host Seahawks trailed the St. Louis Rams 27–20. Seattle was facing a fourth down near the goal line with time running out. Hasselbeck threw a pass to Bobby Engram in the end zone. The ball slipped through the wide receiver's hands, though. The Seahawks lost.

New coach, new league, new quarterback, new stadium—it didn't seem to make any difference. The Seahawks just couldn't seem to get over the hump.

CHAPTER 5

RISING BACK UP

Seattle was tired of falling short in the postseason. The Seahawks had not won a playoff game in 20 years. They entered the 2005 season determined to fix that.

Seattle started 2–2 that year but rallied to win its next 11 games, ending the year with a 13–3 record and home-field advantage throughout the playoffs. Wins over Washington and Carolina launched Seattle into the Super Bowl against Pittsburgh. Despite a remarkable playoff run, the Seahawks fell to the Steelers 21–10.

The Seahawks reached the playoffs again in 2006 and 2007, losing in the second round both years. They went on to win just four games in 2008, touching off another period of transition for the franchise. Holmgren retired from coaching

Running back Shaun Alexander was named the NFL's MVP for the 2005 season.

Riddell
SEAHAWKS
37

Pete Carroll answers questions after he was introduced as the Seahawks' head coach and executive vice president on January 12, 2010.

after that season. Seattle was only slightly better under new coach Jim Mora Jr. in 2009. Mora had been Atlanta's head coach from 2004 to 2006 before going to Seattle. The Seahawks finished just 5–11 in 2009 and Mora was fired.

A new era began that same month when former University of Southern California (USC) coach Pete Carroll was hired to coach the Seahawks. Carroll went 97–19 and won two national titles at USC. His first season in Seattle was an odd one. Hasselbeck threw only 12 touchdown passes and was intercepted 17 times, and both the offense and defense were ranked in the bottom third of the league. The Seahawks finished 7–9, but that was good enough to win a weak division. Seattle's reward was a home playoff game in the first round against the defending Super Bowl champion New Orleans Saints. New Orleans came into the game as a 10-point favorite, even as the road team. But thanks to four Hasselbeck touchdown passes and a huge touchdown run by Marshawn Lynch, the Seahawks pulled off a 41–36 upset.

Hasselbeck was gone after the 2010 season. Seattle struggled to find a quarterback in 2011 and missed the playoffs with a

BEAST QUAKE

Marshawn Lynch joined the Seahawks after a tough start to his NFL career. He had limited success on the field after being drafted by the Buffalo Bills in 2006. Lynch wanted a fresh start and got it when he was traded to Seattle in 2010. He earned the nickname "Beast Mode" for his aggressive running style, which he displayed in the 2010 playoffs against New Orleans. He helped clinch the game when he ran over, around, and through nearly the entire Saints defense on a 67-yard touchdown. The play had the fans so excited that a nearby earthquake sensor registered a small tremor at the stadium.

7–9 record. But in the third round of the 2012 NFL Draft, the Seahawks found their man in Russell Wilson, who overcame doubts about his size and drove Seattle to an 11–5 record as a rookie. After knocking off Washington on the road to open the playoffs, the Seahawks and top-seeded Atlanta met up in an instant classic. Wilson and Lynch led a late touchdown drive to give Seattle a two-point lead. But the Falcons kicked a 49-yard field goal with 13 seconds to play, giving them a 30–28 victory.

The next season was even better for Seattle. The Seahawks went 13–3 for the second time in franchise history and hosted their first two playoff games at their loud home stadium. The fans were supportive throughout as Seattle defeated the San Francisco 49ers in the NFC Championship Game to advance to the Super Bowl. The Seahawks dominated the Broncos in the Super Bowl and were champions for the first time in franchise history.

LEGION OF BOOM

In the early 2010s the Seahawks formed a fearsome secondary. Its core members were cornerback Richard Sherman and safeties Earl Thomas and Kam Chancellor. They helped the Seahawks lead the NFL in fewest points allowed every year from 2012 to 2015. Sherman and Thomas were both first-team All-Pro in three of those years. The players thought they needed a catchy nickname and asked their fans to submit suggestions via Twitter. And that's how "the Legion of Boom" was born.

Seattle came back just as strong in 2014. The Seahawks went 12–4 in the regular season and were back in the NFC Championship Game in their home stadium. This time, the opponents were the Green Bay Packers and star quarterback Aaron Rodgers. Early on, it was all Packers as they took a 16–0 lead at the end of the first half.

The Seahawks didn't score their first touchdown until well into the second half. It happened on a fake field goal when holder Jon Ryan threw to Garry Gilliam to make it 16–7. Still, late in the fourth quarter, the Seahawks trailed 19–7. A rushing touchdown by Wilson made it 19–14 with 2:13 to play. Then the Seahawks recovered an onside kick. Four plays later, Lynch broke free and scored on a 24-yard run. A two-point conversion put Seattle on top 22–19. Green Bay bounced back and kicked a field goal to send the game into overtime. But Wilson threw a game-winning 35-yard touchdown pass to Jermaine Kearse on the first possession. The incredible comeback sent the Seahawks back to the Super Bowl.

Facing the New England Patriots in Super Bowl XLIX, it was Seattle's turn to blow a late lead. Trailing by 10 to start the fourth quarter, the Patriots scored touchdowns on consecutive drives to take a 28–24 lead. The Seahawks got the ball back at their own 20-yard line with 2:02 left. Then Wilson went to work.

Jermaine Kearse (15) makes a juggling catch deep in New England territory on Seattle's final drive of Super Bowl XLIX.

A 31-yard pass to Lynch on the first play of the drive set the tone. Then on third-and-10, Wilson hit receiver Ricardo Lockette for 11 yards. On the next play, Kearse made an amazing, juggling catch at the New England 5-yard line. The Seahawks had moved the ball 75 yards in less than a minute.

On first-and-goal from the 5, Lynch bulled his way to the 1. As one of the NFL's top short-yardage running backs, Lynch appeared to be a cinch to get the ball again on second down. But the Seahawks had other ideas. They tried a quick slant pass to Lockette. But Patriots cornerback Malcolm Butler jumped in front of the receiver and intercepted the pass. The shocking turn of events gave New England the victory. Carroll took the blame for the play call, which was criticized by fans and media who expected to see Lynch run it in.

The Seahawks made the playoffs in 2015 and 2016 but could not get past the second round. The team was beginning to get older, and the roster saw heavy turnover due to retirements and free agency. In 2017, the Seahawks missed the playoffs after going 9–7. Many of the star players that won a Super Bowl had left Seattle.

But Wilson and Carroll remained, leading Seattle to a 10–6 record and a wild-card berth in the NFC playoffs in 2018. A 24–22 loss to the Cowboys in Dallas was a disappointing end to the season, but the Seahawks continue to give their fans hope of more Super Bowl success to come.

TIMELINE

1974
Lloyd W. Nordstrom heads up an ownership group that pays $16 million for a new NFL franchise in Seattle.

1976
The Seahawks go 2–12 in their first season.

1978
Seattle finishes 9–7 with two wins against the Oakland Raiders.

1983
Chuck Knox is named the Seahawks' coach in January.

1984
After winning their first two playoff games, the Seahawks lose to the Los Angeles Raiders in the AFC Championship Game on January 8.

1984
Seattle loses to Dan Marino and the Dolphins in a divisional playoff game on December 29.

1988
The Seahawks win their first division title but lose to the Cincinnati Bengals in the divisional round on December 31.

1991
Knox resigns and is replaced by the team's general manager, Tom Flores.

1995
Former Seahawks wide receiver Steve Largent is inducted into the Pro Football Hall of Fame.

1997
Microsoft cofounder Paul Allen purchases the Seahawks.

1999
Seattle hires former Green Bay Packers coach Mike Holmgren as coach and general manager in January.

2000
The Kingdome is demolished. The Seahawks move into their temporary home at Husky Stadium.

2002
The Seahawks open their new stadium and jump to the NFC.

2006
After rolling through the NFC playoffs, the Seahawks lose 21–10 to the Pittsburgh Steelers in Super Bowl XL on February 5.

2010
Pete Carroll leads the Seahawks to the NFC West title in his first season.

2012
Rookie third-round draft pick Russell Wilson leads Seattle back to the playoffs.

2014
The Seahawks blow out the Denver Broncos 43–8 on February 2 for their first Super Bowl title.

2015
Seattle makes its second consecutive Super Bowl appearance but loses 28–24 to the New England Patriots on February 1.

2018
On October 15, Allen dies at age 65. The NFL says it will ensure that any new owner must agree to keep the team in Seattle.

2018
The Seahawks win six of their last seven games to earn a wild-card playoff spot.

QUICK STATS

FRANCHISE HISTORY

1976–

SUPER BOWLS *(wins in bold)*

2005 (XL), **2013 (XLVIII)**,
2014 (XLIX)

AFC CHAMPIONSHIP GAMES *(1977–2002)*

1983

NFC CHAMPIONSHIP GAMES *(1976, 2003–)*

2005, 2013, 2014

DIVISION CHAMPIONSHIPS *(since 1970 AFL-NFL merger)*

1988, 1999, 2004, 2005, 2006, 2007, 2010, 2013, 2014, 2016

KEY COACHES

Mike Holmgren (1999–2008):
86–74, 4–6 (playoffs)
Chuck Knox (1983–91):
80–63, 3–4 (playoffs)
Pete Carroll (2010–):
89-54-1, 9-6 (playoffs)

KEY PLAYERS *(positions, seasons with team)*

Shaun Alexander (RB, 2000–07)
Dave Brown (DB, 1976–86)
Kenny Easley (S, 1981–87)
Jacob Green (DE, 1980–91)
Matt Hasselbeck (QB, 2001–10)
Walter Jones (OT, 1997–2008)
Cortez Kennedy (DT, 1990–2000)
Dave Krieg (QB, 1980–91)
Steve Largent (WR, 1976–89)
Marshawn Lynch (RB, 2010–15)
Richard Sherman (DB, 2011–17)
Curt Warner (RB, 1983–89)
John L. Williams (FB, 1986–93)
Russell Wilson (QB, 2012–)
Jim Zorn (QB, 1976–84)

HOME FIELDS

CenturyLink Field (2002–)
Also known as Seahawks Stadium, Qwest Field
Husky Stadium (2000–01)
Kingdome (1976–99)

*All statistics through 2018 season

QUOTES AND ANECDOTES

Seattle quarterback Russell Wilson was a bright young star when he joined the NFL in 2012. But he also was highly regarded for his baseball ability. Wilson was drafted by Major League Baseball's Colorado Rockies and played in their minor league system in 2010 and 2011. The Texas Rangers acquired him in 2013. Though he never played for the Rangers, Wilson did show up to the team's spring training in 2014. He later joined the New York Yankees organization and played in a spring training game for the club in 2018.

A name-the-team contest for the Seahawks drew 20,365 entries. Here are some of the potential names Seattle could have had when it joined the NFL: Anchovies, Bumbershoots, Clam Guns, Evergreens, Identified Flying Objects, Sockeyes, and Worms. It was determined that the Seahawks was the most suitable name and made the most sense geographically.

Coach Jack Patera climbed into his car one night. Something did not feel right. He could not tell what until he put the car in gear. The wheels spun, and the car did not move. He realized he had been tricked. "We jacked up the back of his car one night," said Art Kuehn, a former center for the Seahawks. "[Fellow lineman] Nick Bebout and I did it. Then we just sat in the bushes and laughed."

"I'm just here so I won't get fined."

–Response from Seahawks running back Marshawn Lynch, famously distrustful of the media, to every question he was asked at Super Bowl XLIX Media Day, referring to the NFL's policy of requiring players to attend the event

GLOSSARY

berth
A place, spot, or position, such as in the NFL playoffs.

exhibition
A game that doesn't count in the standings.

expansion
The addition of new teams to increase the size of a league.

franchise
A sports organization, including the top-level team and all minor league affiliates.

hall of fame
A place built to honor noteworthy achievements by athletes in their respective sports.

momentum
The sense that a team is playing well and will be difficult to stop.

postseason
The period after the end of a regular season in which additional games or playoffs are held, especially to determine a champion.

prospect
An athlete likely to succeed at the next level.

rookie
A professional athlete in his or her first year of competition.

secondary
The defensive players—cornerbacks and safeties—who start the play farthest from the line.

veteran
A player who has played many years.

wild card
A team that makes the playoffs even though it did not win its division.

MORE INFORMATION

BOOKS

Anderson, Jameson. *Russell Wilson*. Minneapolis, MN: Abdo Publishing, 2015.

Cohn, Nate. *Seattle Seahawks*. New York: AV2 by Weigl, 2018.

Mason, Tyler. *Seattle Seahawks*. Minneapolis, MN: Abdo Publishing, 2017.

ONLINE RESOURCES

Booklinks
NONFICTION NETWORK
FREE! ONLINE NONFICTION RESOURCES

To learn more about the Seattle Seahawks, visit **abdobooklinks.com** or scan this QR code. These links are routinely monitored and updated to provide the most current information available.

PLACES TO VISIT

CenturyLink Field
800 Occidental Ave. S.
Seattle, WA 98134
206-381-7555
centurylinkfield.com

The stadium has a capacity of 67,000 and is the home field of the Seahawks. It also hosts the Seattle Sounders of Major League Soccer.

Virginia Mason Athletic Center
12 Seahawks Way
Renton, WA 98056
425-203-8000
seahawks.com/team/facilities/vmac

This has been the home of the Seahawks' annual training camp along with the team offices since 2008.

INDEX

ABOUT THE AUTHOR

Todd Ryan is a library assistant from the Upper Peninsula of Michigan. He lives near Houghton with his two cats, Izzo and Mooch.